Decodable
READER

UNIT 5

SAVVAS
LEARNING COMPANY

Savvas Learning Company LLC, 15 East Midland Avenue, Paramus, NJ 07652

ISBN-13: 978-0-32-898867-9
ISBN-10:   0-32-898867-7
10 22

Table of Contents

Our State

Written by Leo Albiani

Long o: oa, ow, oe

boats	float	road	soaked
coast	Joe	shows	tow
coats	Moe	snow	

High-Frequency Words

about	some	who
people	there	would
put	what	write

1

There is a prize.

Our State

We like to _____.

We can _____.

The best part_____.

Write what you like best about
our state.
You need to write as a team to win.

Joe and Lee write about when we have snow and ice.
They like to put on their coats.

Moe and Peg write about people who buy beads.
Their art shows a float going down the road.

Fran and Josh write about people
on boats.
The boats are near the coast and
can tow rafts.

Ben and Kim write about fun
on the coast.
Some people get soaked.

Ben and Kim win the prize!
What would you write about
your state?

Wait for Spring

Written by Renée McLean

Three-Letter Consonant Blends

scrap	sprang	spring	sprinted

Long _o_: Vowel Digraph _oa_

boat	coat	loaf	Toad

Long _o_: Vowel Digraph _ow_

pillow	row	showed	snow

Adding Endings (Change _y_ to _i_)

cried	dried	tried

High-Frequency Words

a	said	the	was
come	saw	to	you
have	soon		

9

Toad saw a scrap.
It was a map.
He made a plan.
"I must see Bird!" he cried.

10

Toad sprang up.
He tried to pack his pillow
and a hot loaf.

He sprinted to Bird's home.
"Bird!" he yelled.
"Can you read this map?"

12

Toad showed Bird the map.
"We must row in that boat.
We must follow this map.
We will be rich!"

"But, Toad," said Bird,
"I have jobs at home.
And snow may come soon."

Toad did not like snow.
"That is smart," said Toad.
"We will wait for spring."

Toad stuck the map in his coat.
He went to his snug home.
Then Toad dried his feet by the fire.

Out of Sight

Written by Natasha Bettinger

Long *i*: *igh*

bright	light	night
high	might	sighed

High-Frequency Words

done	put	wash
once	upon	water

17

Once upon a time, a man planted
a seed.
He went to wash his hands.
He hoped the seed might grow.

He put water on the soil each night.

The seed did grow.
The plant was as high as the man!

The man put tall sticks in the soil.
The plant could lean on the sticks.

Soon the plant was up as high as the sky.
The birds cawed with fright!

The plant hid the bright sun.
"It is done growing, but there is
no light," sighed the man.

The man felt a small ball hit
his head.
Peas fell from high in the sky!
He would give peas to all!

Dreams

Written by Victor Rodriguez

Long *i: igh*

high	night
might	sight

Suffix *-or*

actor	inventor
editor	sailor

Suffix *-er*

dancer	trainer
singer	writer
teacher	

High-Frequency Words

done	wash	your
once	water	
upon	what	

What is your dream job?

I dream of being a writer or editor.
My pages will start, "Once upon
a time."

I dream of being a sailor on a boat in the water.

Once I saw sailors on a ship sail
out of sight.

I might be a singer.
I'll sing high notes each night.
When I'm done, the crowd
will cheer.

30

I might be a dog trainer.
I'll wash the dogs.
I'll teach them tricks.

I might be a teacher.
I'll help kids dream big dreams.

The Mix-Up

Written by Noel Vilan

Decodable Reader

53

Vowel Team: *ue, ew, ui*

blue	Drew	Newton
clue	flew	suitcase
cruise	new	swimsuits

High-Frequency Words

because	laugh	off	put	their
here	looks	open	sentence	they

Drew and Ben flew here on a
new jet.
They are going on a cruise.

They go to their room and take off
their coats.
They frown because their suitcases
will not open.

Why won't the blue suitcases open?
They don't have a clue!

They will not let the trip end.
They need to think of a new plan.

Drew looks at the sentence on the tag.
It reads, "This bag is for Ben Newton."

Ben looks at the sentence on the tag.
It reads, "This bag is for Drew Newton."

They laugh because it was a snap
to fix.
They put on swimsuits and go
have fun.

The List

Written by Hector Torres

Prefix: *re-*		
redo	retry	return

Prefix: *un*		
unloads	unlock	unpacks

Vowel Team: *ue, ew, ui*

blue	new
fruit	stew
glue	suit
juice	

High-Frequency Words

because	laugh	open
going	off	sentence

Dad makes a list because he is going to town.
He writes each sentence on the list.

I need a jug of fruit juice.

I need some cans of beans for stew.
I need to get glue to redo the lid
that came off.

I need to return the new blue suit.
It does not fit.

He needs to unlock and open
the trunk.
Then he unloads and unpacks
the cart.

He starts to laugh because he did not return the blue suit.

He will have to retry after lunch!
He opens the beans and starts to
make stew.

A New Game

Written by Sharon Masong

Decodable Reader

55

Long i: i		**Long o: o**	
blindfold	hi	blindfold	hold
child	wind	go	post
		going	told

High-Frequency Words

around	have	move	other
because	house	only	said
eight	learn		

Hi! We are going to learn a game.
We tell each other how to move
in this game.

One child can't see because of
a blindfold.

You must help each other move.
You need to move with care around
the house.

"Hold on to the post," said Ned.
"You only have eight steps to go."

"You told me how to move,"
said Liz.
"Now I will help you move!
Only move when I say to move."

54

"Wind around the blocks," said Liz.
"Stop in eight little steps."

We did well!

Helpful Eve

Written by Eli White

Suffix *-ly*
quickly   safely

Suffix *-ful*
careful   helpful
grateful   useful

Long *i: i*
child   kind

Long *o: o*
fold   holds
goes   most

High-Frequency Words

around   house   little   only   what
eight   learn   move   people

57

Eve is a kind child.
She is only eight.

She is more helpful than most
people.

She quickly goes to her dad
to help him.
Eve likes to be useful around
the house.

She helps little Len learn
to walk safely.
She holds his hand.

Eve is careful.
She helps Mom move the lamp.

She doesn't mind helping Ben
fold shirts.
She quickly finds his lost sock.
He is grateful.

Eve is a kind and helpful child.
If she is this nice at eight, what
will she be like at nine?

64

Time for Bed

Written by Leslie Lin

Syllables V/CV, VC/V

began	never	opened	silent

Vowel Patterns *ow*, *ou*

brow	down	frowned	know	mouth
couch	drowsy	growing	loud	
count	found	howl	low	

High-Frequency Words

behind	to	what
said	was	

"What time is it?" asked Mom.
Ted's brow went up but he
was silent.

66

"Is it time to eat?" asked Ted.
Ted opened his mouth.
"No, it's not time to eat," said Mom.

"Is it time to count?" asked Ted.
"No, it's not time to count,"
said Mom.

"Is it time to hide
and be found?" asked Ted.
Ted hid down low behind the couch.
"No, it's not time to hide," said Mom.

"Is it time to howl?" asked Ted.
Ted began to be loud.
"No, it's never time to howl,"
said Mom.

Ted was growing sleepy.
"I know it's time for bed," he said.
Mom nodded.
Ted frowned.

Ted's lids became drowsy.
"It's time to close my eyes," said Ted.
He went to sleep.

My Youth Troop

Written by Manuel Lopez

Decodable Reader 58

CAMP WEST WORLD

Vowel Team *oo*				**Vowel Team *ou***	
booth	moon	tools	zoom	group	youth
food	room	troop		soup	

High-Frequency Words

look	should	warm	world
put	today	where	years

My youth troop is going camping today.

We go to Camp West World.
The group has camped here
for years.

We packed food to make warm
soup on the campfire.

There isn't much room in the van
for us kids!

We stop at the booth.
They tell us where we should park.

We use tools to put up our tents.
We fill our cups with warm soup.

When it gets dark we tell tales.
We look at the moon and see a star
zoom past.

The Big Game

Written by Rachel Walker

Vowel Sound in *foot*: oo

good	scrapbook	stood
looked	shook	took

Vowel Sound in *foot*: u

full	pushed
put	

High-Frequency Words

another	off	was
father	pictures	what
mother	through	year

This was the last ball game of
the year for Luke.
His mother and father stood on
the sidelines.

The teams pushed through the gate.
Then they shook hands.

The Rams hit the ball first.
Luke was a good catcher.

The ball fell.
Luke picked it up and ran
at full speed.
What a good play!

The Rams hit the ball very high.
Luke put out his arm and looked up.

He got up and shook off the dirt.
Luke would try to catch
another time.

Luke and the Wildcats scored more.
His mother and father took pictures
to put in the scrapbook.

What a Good Year!

Written by Shonda Parr

Final Stable Syllable -le

bundles	sample	table
little	simple	

Vowel Sound in foot: oo

cook	hoods	took
good	stood	wool

Vowel Sound in foot: u

full	put

High-Frequency Words

another	of	together
father	picture	year
mother	through	

89

It was the end of the year.

A man took the last group picture.
The kids all stood by the table with
a big card.

It was a good year!

Kids made books full of pictures.
Each page was a sample of what
they did this year.

Every book was put together as
a gift for a mother or father.

The group learned to cook.
They made simple little hoods
out of bundles of wool.

They waved to one another.
They went through the gate one
last time.